MAY
PEACE AND HAPPINESS
PREVAIL

Keynote Address by
Sri Mata Amritanandamayi Devi
during the Closing Plenary Session of
The Parliament of World's Religions
in Barcelona, Spain, on
July 13th, 2004

MAY PEACE AND HAPPINESS PREVAIL

Published by:
   Mata Amritanandamayi Mission Trust
   Amritapuri P.O., Kollam Dt.,
   Kerala 690 525,India
   E-mail: info@theammashop.org
   Website: www.amritapuri.org

Printed September 2004 - June 2008:
        11,000 copies.
Reprint June 2012: 1000 copies

Typesetting and Layout: Amrita DTP, Amritapuri

CONTENTS

FOREWORD

All together, with a huge prayer, we can change the course of the current events. Each unique human being, who is able to create, is our hope.

Amma advises us: "In our haste, we forget the greatest truth of all – that the source of all problems is to be found within the human mind." As in the verse of the great American writer Archibald McLeish, with which begins the splendid preamble of the radiant Constitution of UNESCO: "Since war is born from the mind of human beings, it is in the mind of human beings that we must erect the castle of peace."

The real education frees and permits us to act according to our own decisions, without following the dictates of anyone. The mass media, so useful, can also, by its omnipresence and attractive power, convert us into passive spectators, making us all identical, and docile before what they offer, making us acquiesce to their self-serving recommendations. It is essential to have time to think, to feel, to listen, to get to know others, and finally – and this is very difficult – to get to know our own selves.

As Amma said in the Parliament of World Religions, "Along with an understanding of the outer world, it is essential that we also get to know the inner world." She added, "Love and compassion are the very essence of all religions... Love has no limitations such as religion, race, nationality, or caste."

To eradicate poverty, to alleviate or somehow wipe away the suffering! For this, it is necessary to give, and to give oneself. To give all that we can, but above all, to give our time. Our knowledge, our brotherhood.

The material poverty of many people is the result of the spiritual poverty of those who could have given them relief. It should be urgently emphasized that this is the result of a culture of force, of imposition, of domination. And a result of the people and institutions that remain quiet instead of freely expressing their protests and proposals.

The moment has arrived for the culture of dialogue, of mutual agreement, of understanding. The moment has arrived for the culture of peace, the culture of the helping hand, of the united voices. At last, the century of the people! At last, all distinct, but all united! Thus will begin a new step in the history of mankind.

Amma asks that we work in favor of others, for the most needy. I wish that Her prayer be granted: "May the tree of our life be firmly rooted in the soil of love."

Federico Mayor Zaragoza
Ex-Secretary General of UNESCO
President of Fundación Cultura de Paz
(Foundation Culture of Peace),
Madrid, Spain
August 2004

INTRODUCTION

Nowadays, we often associate concepts like diversity and differences of religion and culture with conflict, war, and terrorism. The world has changed since September 11, 2001; our collective consciousness has become filled with fear, suspicion, and even hostility toward those who are different from us. At this moment in history, an international interfaith gathering is perhaps more essential than ever before. The world is thirsting for a voice that inspires us to unite in peace. At the 2004 Parliament of the World's Religions in Barcelona, Amma was this voice. The universal and timeless wisdom of Her words speaks to us, and reaches us, with an extraordinary vibrancy at this critical time.

The moment Amma walked onto the stage, the entire audience stood up and

cheered. One newspaper reporter said: "Her personality is such that one feels a spontaneous attraction toward Her. And She is, of course, different and unique, not like other spiritual masters." The hall was filled to capacity, with people over-flowing into the aisles and corridors. One could feel the air permeated with deep reverence and uncontainable excitement. Amma was to give the keynote address during the closing plenary session of the seven-day parliament. Her theme was "Pathways to Peace—the Wisdom of Listening, the Power of Commitment." What teaching would this remarkable spiritual being bestow on the occasion? How would She synthesize the essence of the hundreds of lectures, discussions, and symposia presented throughout this event into a single, integrated, unifying message? As Amma spoke, the answer came. The real problems that we face today, and ways to resolve them, were laid out one by one. Amma was able to bring together all messages, teachings and paths into one, as this is the role of the true spiritual master. As always, Her words were simple, though profound. Ex-pressing the deepest spiritual principles, Amma's speech contained engaging stories, practical examples and beautiful analogies. She managed to touch on virtually all areas of life in Her brief, yet powerful speech.

Amma's speech begins by explaining how to look upon our God-given talents. By increasing our innate spiritual power, rather than just power in its various material forms, we can achieve real peace and contentment. Instead of merely blaming religion for the perpetual frustration humanity faces in its search for happiness, the speech provides a fresh view on religion and spirituality, a view that is badly needed in today's world. Exhorting all to see and to understand the essence of religion from a spiritual perspective, Amma reminds us, "Where there is true spiritual experience, there will be no division – only unity and love."

Warning against religious bigotry, Amma notes, "The problem arises when we say, 'Our religion is right; yours is wrong!' This is like saying, 'My mother is good; yours is a prostitute!'" But She also points out the way to a solution: "Love is the only religion that can help humanity rise to great and glorious heights. And love should be the one thread on which all religions and philosophies are strung together." She goes on to say that to awaken unity and to spread love requires that we respect diversity and listen to others with an open heart.

Amma also beautifully addresses the subject of war, advocating that we redirect the money and effort spent on war toward world peace instead, and suggesting that this "could definitely bring about peace and harmony in this world." Here, again, She stresses that the key to overcoming both the internal and external enemies is not physical or ideological coercion, but spirituality.

Amma continues by redefining the notion of another of today's global dilemmas – poverty. Dividing poverty into two kinds, physical and spiritual, Amma urges us all to give priority to addressing the latter, as only such an approach can provide a lasting solution to both.

Amma's teachings always take us beyond our personal differences and desires, leading us to experience humanity's underlying unity. In Barcelona, She again emphasizes this message of unity in the culmination of Her speech. In telling a touching story about a rainbow, Amma illustrates how diversity and unity can coexist, if we can only gain the wisdom of finding our own happiness in making others happy.

Amma has said so often that serving the poor is our supreme duty to God, and in concluding this speech She calls for a clear commitment from Her children, saying, "We should commit ourselves to working an extra half-hour a day for the sake of those who are suffering – this is Amma's request." Who else is more qualified to speak on the importance and beauty of selfless service? Such words carry an entirely different dimension of persuasiveness when coming from one who has so masterfully sculpted Her life so that it is an image of Her own teachings.

Amma's speech was followed by thunderous applause and a standing ovation.

That night, although it was not a part of the original program (in fact, the Parliament had ended), Amma gave darshan. A huge crowd of admirers and a number of officials and delegates of the conference came for Her blessing.

The darshan took place in a tent overlooking the Mediterranean Sea. This tent had been erected by the Sikh community to feed the Parliament delegates. Amma arrived at the tent shortly after leaving the Parliament, and unceremoniously walked to a chair that had been set in place minutes before (for no one had been sure that She would be giving darshan). With no ado whatsoever, She began receiving people in Her unique way of embracing everyone, and within minutes, despite the absence of a sound system, people began singing bhajans, and everyone joined in. The darshan, which continued late into the night, seemed to be a manifestation of what Amma's speech a few hours before had called for: here were people from all over Europe, all over the world, and from different religions, all joining together in the experience of love. Diversity brought together into unity – the basis for peace.

During the night, the Sikh leader along with a big group of his followers came to honor Amma. Speaking words of reverence and welcome, he reached both hands into a large bowl, bringing them out overflowing with flower petals, and exuberantly showered them to Amma. She responded by taking the petals in Her hands, and showering them on him and his followers.

And then, nothing less than a miracle took place. Amma became concerned because people had been with Her for so many hours and nobody had eaten anything. The Sikhs offered what they had left: enough food for perhaps 150 meals. When darshan ended, Amma went directly to the serving tables and began serving food to Her children. Now and then, She would adjust the serving portions of one item or another, calculating precisely to be sure that everyone would be fed. And She succeeded, for in the end everyone was served an ample meal, all the pots had been scraped clean, and there was no waste. How food for one hundred and fifty fed over a thousand, leaving no one hungry and no food wasted, cannot be explained.

Within a few hours of finishing darshan and feeding Her children, Amma was again at the airport, less than twenty-four hours from the time of Her arrival. The Parliament occurred while Amma was on Her annual U.S. Tour. She left at the end of the Chicago program, gave Her speech and the impromptu darshan, and returned in time for Her next program, in Washington, D.C.

Barcelona set yet another stage for Amma's never-ending message of Love. Indeed, Love conquers everything. So let us, too, open our hearts and surrender to that Love. The words of a *mahatma* [great soul] are like seeds sown in the soil of our hearts. If the soil is receptive and nurtures the seeds, they can produce great trees, giving fruit and shade to many people in need. May Amma's words germinate and grow in our hearts, making our lives fruitful and beneficial for the world.

As I conclude these words, let me recall a quote from an article that appeared in one of the mainstream Spanish newspapers, *el Periódico*: "Amma is a good spiritual ace in a world that is lacking faith."

Yes, She truly leads us to the ultimate success, which is to go beyond all weaknesses of the mind, realize our full potential, and eventually attain peace and tranquility in all circumstances of life.

Swami Amritaswarupananda Puri
Vice-Chairman
Mata Amritanandamayi Math
Amritapuri

Keynote Address by
Sri Mata Amritanandamayi Devi
during the Closing Plenary Session of
The Parliament of World's Religions
in Barcelona, Spain, on
July 13th, 2004

Amma bows down to everyone who is truly the embodiment of pure love and the Supreme Consciousness. The effort and self-sacrifice of those amongst you who were capable of organizing an enormous event such as this are beyond description. Amma simply bows down before such selflessness.

Our God-given abilities are a treasure that is meant for ourselves as well as for the entire world. This wealth should never be misused and made into a burden for us and for the world. The greatest tragedy in life is not death; the greatest tragedy is to let our great potential, talents, and capabilities be underutilized, to allow them to rust while we live. When we use the wealth obtained from nature, it diminishes; but when we use the wealth of our inner gifts, it increases.

But are we really using our abilities?

What has always been the aim of humanity? What do we humans yearn to reach? Has it not always been our goal to obtain as much happiness and contentment as possible in both our personal lives and for society as a whole? But where do we stand today? Most of us move from one mistake to another, which only makes our problems worse.

Every country has tried to increase its power in politics, the military and weaponry, economics, science, and technology. Is there any area we have yet to test and explore? We are all so focused on these things; and having tried these methods for so long, have we achieved any real peace or contentment? The answer is no. Time has proven that these methods alone cannot secure our contentment. Only if spiritual power—with which we have never before experimented—is allowed to grow alongside all those different areas, can we attain the peace and contentment that we seek.

In reality, there is only one difference between people in wealthy countries and people in poor countries: while people in wealthy countries are crying in air-conditioned rooms and palatial mansions, those who live in poor countries are crying on the dirt floors of their huts. One thing is clear: that people who once had every hope to smile and be happy are now shedding tears in many parts of the world. Sorrow and suffering are becoming the hallmark of many countries. It is senseless to blame all this on religion alone. A major cause of these problems is how people have *interpreted* religion and spirituality.

Today we search outwardly for the causes and solutions to all the problems of the world. In our haste, we forget the greatest truth of all—that the source of all problems is to be found within the human mind. We forget that the world can become good only if the mind of the individual becomes good. So, along with an understanding of the outer world, it is essential that we also get to know the inner world.

There was once a function to inaugurate a new supercomputer. After the inauguration, the participants were told they could ask the supercomputer any question and it would come up with the answer in seconds. People did their best to ask the computer the most complicated questions relating to science, history, geography, and so on. As soon as each question was posed, the answer would pop up on the screen. Then, a child stood up and asked the supercomputer a simple question: "Hello, supercomputer! How are you today?" But this time there was no response; the screen remained blank! The computer could answer questions about everything, except itself.

Most of us live in a state similar to that of the computer. Along with our understanding of the outer world, we need to develop knowledge about the inner world.

When our phone is out of order, we call the phone company to repair it; when our cable TV fails to clearly receive TV programs, the cable company helps us; and when our Internet connection isn't working, a computer expert fixes it. In a similar way, spirituality is the means by which our inner connection with the Divine is restored. The science of spirituality puts the 'remote control' of our mind back into our hands.

There are two types of education: education for a living and education for life. When we study in college, striving to become a doctor, a lawyer, or an engineer, that is education for a living. But education for life requires an understanding of the essential principles of spirituality; it is about gaining a deeper understanding of the world, our minds, our emotions, and ourselves. We all know that the real goal of education is not to create people who understand only the language of machines; the main purpose of education should be to impart a *culture of the heart,* a culture based on spiritual values.

Viewing religion only outwardly creates more and more division. We need to see and understand the inside, the *essence* of religion, from a spiritual perspective. Only then will the sense of division come to an end. Where there is division, there cannot be any real spiritual experience; and where there is true spiritual experience, there will be no division—only unity and love. Religious leaders should be prepared to work on the basis of this knowledge, and make their followers aware of these truths.

The problem arises when we say, "Our religion is right; yours is wrong!" This is like saying, "My mother is good; yours is a prostitute!" Love and compassion are the very essence of all religions. What, then, is the need for us to compete?

Love is our true essence. Love has no limitations such as religion, race, nationality, or caste. We are all beads strung

21

together on the same thread of love. To awaken this unity and to spread the love that is our inherent nature to others—this is the true aim of human life.

Indeed, love is the only religion that can help humanity rise to great and glorious heights. And love should be the one thread on which all religions and philosophies are strung together. The beauty of society lies in the unity of hearts.

There is so much diversity in *Sanatana Dharma*, India's ancient spiritual tradition. Every person is unique and has a different mental constitution. The seers of old provided us with a multitude of paths, so that each individual could choose the way most suitable for him or her. All locks cannot be opened with the same key; nor does everyone like the same type of food or clothing. This diversity holds equally true for spirituality. The same path is not suitable for everyone.

Meetings and conferences such as this need to place more emphasis on spirituality, on the inner essence of religion. This is the only way to achieve peace and unity. This conference shouldn't be just a meeting of bodies. On an occasion such as this, a true meeting should take place, one in which we can see and know each other's hearts.

Communication through machines has made people in distant places seem very close. Yet, because of the lack of communication of our hearts, even those who are physically close to us can seem very far away.

So, this should not be an ordinary conference, where everyone talks, nobody listens, and everyone disagrees!

Listening to each other is important. We may see and hear many things in the world, but we shouldn't meddle in the affairs of others because that can have dangerous consequences. Amma remembers a story.

A man walked past a mental hospital when he heard a voice groaning, "13, 13, 13, 13..." The man went closer to locate where the sound was coming from. He saw a hole in the wall and realized that the sound was coming from the other side. Out of curiosity, he put his ear into the hole, hoping to hear better. Suddenly, something bit him hard on the ear! As he screamed in pain, the voice groaned, "14, 14, 14, 14..."!

Thus, we should use our power of discrimination to distinguish between what we should or should not pay attention to.

True religious leaders love and even worship the whole of creation, seeing everything as God-consciousness. They see the unity underlying all diversity. But, nowadays, many religious leaders misinterpret the words and experiences of the ancient seers and prophets, and they exploit weak-minded people.

Religion and spirituality are the keys with which we can open our hearts and see everyone with compassion. But our minds, being blinded by selfishness, have lost their proper judgment; our vision has become distorted. And this attitude will only serve to create more darkness. Using that very same key that is meant to open our hearts, our indiscriminate mindset locks our hearts shut instead.

There is a story about four men who were on their way to attend a religious conference and had to spend the night together on an island. It was a bitter-cold night. Each traveler carried a matchbox and a small bundle of firewood in his pack, but each one thought he was the only one who had firewood and matches.

One of them thought, "Judging from the medallion around that man's neck, I would say he is from some other religion. If I start a fire, he will also benefit from the warmth. Why should I use my precious wood to warm him?"

The second man thought, "That person is from the country that has always fought against us. I wouldn't dream of using my wood to make him comfortable!"

The third man looked at one of the others and thought, "I know that fellow. He belongs to a sect that always creates problems in my religion. I'm not going to waste my wood for his sake!"

The fourth man thought, "That man has a different skin color and I hate that! There's no way I'm going to use my wood for him!"

In the end, not one of them was willing to light his wood to warm the others, and so, by morning, they all froze to death. Similarly, we harbor enmity toward others in the name of religion, nationality, color, and caste, without showing any compassion toward our fellow beings.

Modern society is like a person suffering from a severe fever. As the fever increases, the person utters words that make no sense. Pointing at a chair on the floor, she may say, "Oh, the chair is talking to me! Look, it's flying!" How can we respond? Is it possible to prove to her that the chair isn't flying? There's only one way to help her: we have to give her the necessary medicine to bring down the fever, and once the fever is reduced, everything will return to normal. Today, people are suffering from the fever of selfishness, greed, unrestrained desire, etc.

Religion and spirituality form the path that helps to transform the anger within us into compassion, our hatred into love, our lustful thoughts into divine thoughts, and our jealousy into sympathy. Yet, in our present deluded mental state, most of us do not understand this.

Society is comprised of individuals. It is the conflict in the individual mind that manifests outwardly as war. When individuals change, society will automatically change. Just as hatred and vengefulness exist in the mind, peace and love can also exist in the mind.

To wage wars, we spend billions of dollars and engage countless people. Think of how much attention and intense effort go into that process! If we were to use even a fraction of that money and effort for the sake of world peace, we could definitely bring about peace and harmony in this world.

Every country spends huge amounts on building security systems. Security is indispensable; but the greatest security of all comes when we imbibe the spiritual principles and live accordingly. We have forgotten this.

Today the enemies that are attacking us from both within and without cannot be dealt with just by increasing the power of our weapons. We can no longer afford to delay the rediscovery and strengthening of our most powerful weapon, spirituality, which is inherent in us all.

There are over a billion people in this world suffering from poverty and starvation. Poverty, in truth, is our greatest enemy. It is one of the basic reasons why people commit theft and murder, and why people become terrorists. It is also the reason why people turn to prostitution. Poverty not only affects the body, but also weakens the mind. And such minds are then influenced in the name of religion and injected with the poison of terrorist ideals. Looking at it this way, Amma feels that 80% of the problems in society would be resolved if we were to eradicate poverty.

In general, the human race is on a journey without a clear goal.

A driver pulled up to an intersection and asked a pedestrian, "Could you tell me where this road leads to?"

"Where do you want to go?" asked the pedestrian.

"I don't know," replied the driver.

"Well, then," said the pedestrian, "it obviously doesn't matter which road you take!"

We shouldn't be like that driver. We need to have a clear goal.

Amma is alarmed to see the direction in which the world is heading. If, in the future, there is a third world war, let it not be a war between nations, but a war against our common enemy, poverty!

In today's world, people experience two types of poverty: the poverty caused by lack of food, clothing, and shelter, and the poverty caused by lack of love and compassion. Of these two, the second type needs to be considered first—because, if we have love and compassion in our hearts, then we will wholeheartedly serve those who suffer from lack of food, clothing, and shelter.

It is not the era we live in, but the compassionate hearts that will bring about a change in society. And religions should be able to create more compassionate hearts. This should be the main objective of religion and spirituality.

In order to protect this world, we have to choose a path by which we forsake our personal differences and desires. By forgiving and forgetting, we can try to recreate and give new life to this world. It is useless to dig up and scrutinize the past; it won't benefit anyone. We need to abandon the path of vengeance and retaliation, and impartially evaluate the present world situation. Only then can we discover the path to true progress.

True unity—amongst people and between humanity and nature—will come only through our faith in the immense power of the inner Self, which is beyond all outward differences.

A rainbow gives us visual splendor and also has an inner significance that helps to expand the mind. A rainbow is formed by the convergence of seven different colors, making it wondrous and beautiful. Similarly, we should be able to accept and appreciate the differences created by religion, nationality, language, and culture. We should join hands, giving primary importance to the well-being of humanity and universal human values.

A rainbow appears and disappears in the sky within minutes. However, within that short span of time, the rainbow is able to make everyone happy. Just like the rainbow, which appears so briefly in the infinite sky, our lifespan, which appears for just a brief moment within the endless span of time, is also very short and insignificant. As long as we live in this world, our greatest and foremost duty, or *dharma,* is to be of some benefit to others. Only when goodness awakens within the individual will his or her personality and actions attain beauty and strength.

There was once a little girl who was confined to a wheelchair. Her disability made her angry and frustrated with life. All day long, she would sit by her window feeling depressed, enviously watching all the other little children as they ran, jumped, skipped, and played with each other. One day, as she sat gazing through the window, it began to drizzle. Suddenly, a beautiful rainbow appeared in the sky. Instantly, the little girl forgot about her disability and her sorrow. The rainbow filled her with so much happiness and hope. But then, just as suddenly as it had appeared, the drizzle stopped and the rainbow vanished. The memory of the rainbow filled the girl with a strange peace and joy. She asked her mother where the rainbow had gone. Her mother answered, "My darling, rainbows are very special creations. They exist only when the sun and rain come together." From then on, the little girl would sit by her window, waiting for the sun and the rain to come together. She no longer cared to watch the other children play. Finally, one bright day, it unexpectedly began to rain lightly, and the most heavenly-colored rainbow appeared in the sky. The little girl's joy knew no bounds. She called out to her mother to come quickly and take her to the rainbow. Not wanting to disappoint her child, the mother helped her into the car and drove off in the direction of the rainbow. Finally, when they arrived at a point where they had a good view of the rainbow, the mother stopped the car and helped her daughter to get out so that she could enjoy the sight.

Gazing up, the child said, "Wondrous rainbow, how is it that you are able to shine so radiantly?"

The rainbow replied, "My dear child, I have a very short lifespan. I exist only for a brief span of time while the sun and rain come together. Rather than fret over my short existence, I decided that within my brief lifespan, I want to make as many people as I can as happy as possible. And when I decided to do that, I became radiant and beautiful."

Then, even as the rainbow was still speaking, it began to fade—until, finally, it was no more. The little girl looked up with love and admiration at the spot in the blue sky where the rainbow had just been. From that day on, she was never the same. Instead of feeling dejected and fretting about her disability, she tried to smile and bring happiness to everyone around her. Thus, she found true joy and satisfaction in life.

The rainbow was so beautiful because it forgot about itself and lived for the sake of others. Similarly, it is when we forget about ourselves and live for the happiness of others that we experience the real beauty of life.

The body will perish whether we work or sit idle. So, instead of rusting away without doing anything for society, it is better to wear oneself out in the pursuit of good actions.

In *Sanatana Dharma*—the Eternal

Religion (commonly known today as Hinduism)—there is the following mantra: "*Lokah Samastha Sukhino Bhavantu.*" The meaning of this mantra is "May all beings in all the worlds be happy."

According to the scriptures of India, there is no difference between the Creator and creation, just as there is no difference between the ocean and its waves. The essence of the ocean and its waves is one and the same: it is water. Gold and gold ornaments are the same because gold is the substance of which the ornaments are made. Clay and the clay pot are ultimately the same because the substance of the pot is clay. So, there is no difference between the Creator, or God, and creation. They are essentially one and the same: Pure Consciousness. So, we should learn to love everyone equally, because in essence we are all one, the *atman;* we are all one soul or Self. Though outwardly everything appears different, inwardly all are manifestations of the Absolute Self.

God is not a limited individual who sits alone up in the clouds on a golden throne. God is the Pure Consciousness that dwells within everything. We need to understand this truth, and thereby learn to accept and to love everyone equally.

Just as the sun doesn't need the light of a candle, God doesn't need anything from us. God is the Giver of everything. We should move among the suffering people and serve them.

There are millions of refugees and destitute people in the world. Governments are trying to help such people in various ways, but the world needs far more people who are willing to work in a spirit of selflessness.

At the hands of self-serving people, one million dollars becomes only 100,000 dollars by the time the money reaches the people who should benefit from those funds. It is like pouring oil from one container into another and then into another and so forth. After doing this many times, there is no oil left because some of it sticks to each container. But with those who are engaged in selfless service, it is quite different. Such people may receive hundreds of thousands of dollars but will deliver the equivalent of millions to people in need. This is because their motives are selfless; they simply desire to benefit society. Rather than take any pay for themselves, they give all they can to those who are suffering.

If we have at least a little compassion in our hearts, we should commit ourselves to work an extra half hour a day for the sake of those who are suffering—this is Amma's request. Amma believes that in this way a solution to all the sorrow and the poverty in the world will be revealed.

Today's world needs people who express goodness in their words and deeds. If such noble role models can set an example for their fellow beings, the darkness now prevailing in society will be dispelled, and the light of peace and non-violence will once again illumine this earth. Let us work together toward this goal.

> *May the tree of our life be firmly rooted in the soil of love;*
> *Let good deeds be the leaves on that tree;*
> *May words of kindness form its flowers;*
> *And may peace be its fruits.*

Let us grow and unfold as one family, united in love so that we may rejoice and celebrate our oneness in a world where peace and contentment prevail.

As Amma concludes Her words, She would also like to add that, in truth, nothing is the end. Just like the period at the end of a sentence, there is only a short pause—a pause before a new beginning on the path to peace. May divine Grace bless us with the strength to carry forth this message.

Aum Shanti Shanti Shanti.

Book Catalog
By Author

Sri Mata Amritanandamayi Devi
108 Quotes On Faith
108 Quotes On Love
Compassion, The Only Way To Peace:
    Paris Speech
Cultivating Strength And Vitality
Living In Harmony
May Peace And Happiness Prevail:
    Barcelona Speech
May Your Hearts Blossom:
    Chicago Speech
Practice Spiritual Values And Save The
    World: Delhi Speech
The Awakening Of Universal
    Motherhood: Geneva Speech
The Eternal Truth
The Infinite Potential Of Women:
    Jaipur Speech
Understanding And Collaboration
    Between Religions
Unity Is Peace: Interfaith Speech

Swami Amritaswarupananda Puri
Ammachi: A Biography
Awaken Children, Volumes 1-9
From Amma's Heart
Mother Of Sweet Bliss
The Color Of Rainbow

Swami Jnanamritananda Puri
Eternal Wisdom, Volumes 1-2

Swami Paramatmananda Puri
On The Road To Freedom Volumes 1-2
Talks, Volumes 1-6

Swami Purnamritananda Puri
Unforgettable Memories

Swami Ramakrishnananda Puri
Eye Of Wisdom
Racing Along The Razor's Edge
Secret Of Inner Peace
The Blessed Life
The Timeless Path
Ultimate Success

Swamini Krishnamrita Prana
Love Is The Answer
Sacred Journey
The Fragrance Of Pure Love
Torrential Love

M.A. Center Publications
1,000 Names Commentary
Archana Book (Large)
Archana Book (Small)
Being With Amma
Bhagavad Gita
Bhajanamritam, Volumes 1-6
Embracing The World
For My Children
Immortal Light
Lead Us To Purity
Lead Us To The Light
Man And Nature
My First Darshan
Puja: The Process Of Ritualistic
    Worship
Sri Lalitha Trishati Stotram

Amma's Websites

AMRITAPURI—Amma's Home Page
Teachings, Activities, Ashram Life, eServices, Yatra, Blogs and News
http://www.amritapuri.org

AMMA (Mata Amritanandamayi)
About Amma, Meeting Amma, Global Charities, Groups and Activities and Teachings
http://www.amma.org

EMBRACING THE WORLD®
Basic Needs, Emergencies, Environment, Research and News
http://www.embracingtheworld.org

AMRITA UNIVERSITY
About, Admissions, Campuses, Academics, Research, Global and News
http://www.amrita.edu

THE AMMA SHOP—Embracing the World® Books & Gifts Shop
Blog, Books, Complete Body, Home & Gifts, Jewelry, Music and Worship
http://www.theammashop.org

IAM—Integrated Amrita Meditation Technique®
Meditation Taught Free of Charge to the Public, Students, Prisoners and Military
http://www.amma.org/groups/north-america/projects/iam-meditation-classes

AMRITA PUJA
Types and Benefits of Pujas, Brahmasthanam Temple, Astrology Readings, Ordering Pujas
http://www.amritapuja.org

GREENFRIENDS
Growing Plants, Building Sustainable Environments, Education and Community Building
http://www.amma.org/groups/north-america/projects/green-friends

FACEBOOK
This is the Official Facebook Page to Connect with Amma
https://www.facebook.com/MataAmritanandamayi

DONATION PAGE
Please Help Support Amma's Charities Here:
http://www.amma.org/donations

www.ingramcontent.com/pod-product-compliance
Lightning Source LLC
Chambersburg PA
CBHW051000030426
42339CB00007B/411